현지어와 함께 떠나는 어린이여행인문학 ㉓ 대한민국

제주도에서 태양을 보다

박정경 **지음** | 이은미 **그림**
초판 인쇄일 2020년 4월 17일 | **초판 발행일** 2020년 5월 1일
펴낸이 조기룡 | **펴낸곳** 내인생의책 | **등록번호** 제10호-2315호
주소 서울특별시 성동구 연무장5가길 7 현대테라스타워 E동 1403호
전화 02)335-0449, 335-0445(편집) | **팩스** 02)6499-1165
전자 우편 bookinmylife@naver.com | **홈페이지** http://bookinmylife.com

ISBN 979-11-5723-610-7(77810)
　　　979-11-5723-396-0(세트)

* 책값은 뒤표지에 있습니다.
* 잘못된 책은 구입처에서 바꾸어 드립니다.

이 도서의 국립중앙도서관 출판예정도서목록(CIP)은 서지정보유통지원시스템 홈페이지(http://seoji.nl.go.kr)와
국가자료종합목록 구축시스템(http://kolis-net.nl.go.kr)에서 이용하실 수 있습니다. (CIP제어번호 : CIP2020011512)

내인생의책에서는 참신한 발상, 따뜻한 시선을 가진 원고를 기다리고 있습니다.
원고는 나무의 목숨값에 해당하는 가치를 지녔으면 합니다.
원고는 내인생의책 전자 우편이나 홈페이지를 이용해 보내 주세요.

어린이제품 안전 특별법에 의한 제품 표시
세소자명 내인생의책 | **제조 연월** 2020년 4월 | **제조국** 대한민국 | **사용연령** 5세 이상
주소 및 연락처 서울특별시 성동구 연무장5가길 7 현대테라스타워 E동 1403호 02)335-0449

I See the Sun In Jeju Island

제주도에서 태양을 보다

박정경 지음 | **이은미** 그림

박정경 지음

아이들에게 파란 하늘과 마음껏 뛰어놀 수 있는 초록 들판을 선물해 주고 싶어 제주도에서 살고 있습니다. 내일은 오늘과 또 다른 새로운 세상이 열린다는 생각으로 꿋꿋하게 살아가는, 아직 세상은 충분히 살아 볼 만한 가치가 있다고 생각하는 한 사람입니다. 지은 책으로는 《엄마는 너를 위해》가 있습니다.

이은미 그림

연세대학교에서 영문학을 전공하고, 한국영화아카데미에서 애니메이션 연출을 공부했습니다. 단편 애니메이션 〈In Your Eyes〉, 장편 애니메이션 〈제불찰씨 이야기〉를 연출하고 〈로망은 없다〉〈집〉 등의 장편 애니메이션의 미술 작업에 참여했습니다. 《상사가 없는 월요일》《프라하》《혈안》 등의 책 표지들과 《반구대 암각화 이야기》《우리 조상의 유배 이야기》《바다 쓰레기의 비밀》 등의 어린이 그림책을 그렸습니다. 현재 네이버 그라폴리오(http://grafolio.com/_enid)에서 활동하며 〈엄마의 스케치북〉이라는 스토리를 연재 중입니다.

Written by Park Jung-Kyung

I live in Jeju Island because I want to give my children a place with blue skies and green fields where they can frolic to their hearts' desire. I am a person who lives with the strong belief that tomorrow, a new world, better than today will come, and the thought that the world is still worth living in. Another book by this author:《For you, Mom》

Illustrated by Lee Eun-mi

I've drawn for a number of various projects including animation, book cover illustration, promotional illustration, and more and have illustrated children's picture books like 《The Story of Bangudae Petroglyph Rock》《The Tales of Our Ancestor's Banishment》《The Secrets of the Sea Trash》 and 《Looking at the Sun in Lapland》. I'm publishing a series of stories called "Mother's Sketchbook" on NAVER Graflio(http://grafolio.com/_enid).

자연과 문화유산이 아름다운 제주,
그 본연의 힘으로 오랫동안 이어지고 지켜지길 바라며

Jeju, with beautiful nature and cultural heritage
May it continue and be kept for a long time on its strength.

내인생의책

Tweet, Tweet

My eyes are opened to the clear sound of birds.
The sun is slowly climbing up
over my forehead.

삐오오롱, 삐오오롱.

낭랑한 새소리에 눈을 떠요.
이마 위로 햇살이 슬그머니 다가오네요.

My mom gets ready to go to Grandma's house early in the morning.
She puts sea urchin seaweed soup in a finely wrapped picnic box.
There is also a seasoned dried bracken salad that I picked with
my grandmother in the spring.

Ah! Today is my grandmother's birthday.
I'm going over to my grandmother's house and eat breakfast
then we'll thin out the tangerines together.

엄마가 아침 일찍부터 할머니 댁에 갈 준비를 해요.
곱게 싼 찬합에 성게 미역국을 넣었어요.
봄에 할머니랑 같이 딴 고사리로 만든 무침도 있어요.

아! 오늘은 할머니 생신이지요.
할머니 댁에 가서 아침을 먹고 함께 귤을 솎을 거예요.

In May, the tangerine flowers that filled the whole island with beautiful fragrances fade, and when the dripping little tangerines start forming, my grandmother and grandfather's hands get busy.

My family goes to my grandmother's house every weekend to help with the tangerine farm. The tangerine trees are flush with tangerines jostling lightly in the wind. To get big and delicious tangerines, you have to weed out the small and weak ones.

5월에 섬 전체를 향기로운 꽃 내음으로 가득 채웠던 귤꽃이 지고
방울방울 작은 귤이 열리기 시작하면, 할머니와 할아버지의 손이 바빠져요.

우리 가족은 주말마다 할머니 댁에 가서 귤 농사를 도와요.
귤나무에는 조그만 아기 귤이 **와랑와랑** 달려 있어요.
크고 맛있는 귤을 얻기 위해서는 작고 약한 귤을 따 줘야 한대요.

"Grandmother, why do you keep picking tangerines?
These baby ones would get bigger if we left them alone, it's such a waste."
I pick up and embrace the fallen tangerines and ask.

"When tangerines hang in a cluster like this, it is tough for the trees,
Many of them are spoiled and rotten as well, so you have to pick them out
when they are little. Then the rest of the tangerines quickly grow
bigger and are much better for selling."

She told me this while teaching me how to peel tangerines,
but I'm still upset about throwing them away.

"할머니, 왜 귤을 자꾸 따요? 아기 귤도 놔두면 크게 자랄 텐데 아까워요."
바닥으로 떨어진 귤을 손 한가득 주워 안고 물어요.

"이렇게 자락자락 귤이 달리민 **낭도 버치고** 개중엔 병든 것,
상한 것 섞여 이서 어릴 때 미리 따 부러사 나머지 귤들이
무락무락 컹 상품이 되는 거여."

할머니가 귤 솎는 걸 가르쳐 주며 말했지만
나는 그래도 귤을 떨구는 게 속상해요.

* "이렇게 주렁주렁 귤이 달리면 나무도 힘들고,
개중엔 병든 것, 상한 것이 섞여 있어 어릴 때 미리 따 버려야
나머지 귤들이 무럭무럭 커서 상품이 되는 거야."

Snap! Snap! Crack.
Every time I pick a tangerine, "Ouch, Ouch!"
I hear them screaming out in pain.

"My goodness, I'm tired. As I get older, my body gets tired,
my knees hurt, my back feels like it's going to break.
I can't even farm tangerines anymore. If I still had my older brother."

When grandma's having a hard time, she talks about her big brother.
My grandma's brother went missing
during the April 4·3 incident on Jeju Island.

딱! 딱! 후드득.
귤을 딸 때마다 "아야, 아야!"
귤이 아프다고 말하는 것만 같아요.

"아이고, 버쳐. 늙어가난 몸도 버치고 종애도 아프고, 허리도 그차질 거 닮고
이젠 귤 농시도 못 해 먹주게. 오라방이라도 아즉 있었으민."

할머니는 힘들 때면 큰할아버지 이야기를 해요.
할머니의 오빠는 제주 4·3 사건 때 행방불명되었대요.

* "아이고, 힘들어. 늙어가니 몸도 힘들고 무릎도 아프고, 허리도 끊어질 거 같고
이제 귤 농사도 못 해 먹겠다. 오빠라도 아직 있었으면."

"Eat Lunch!"
My mom calls from the cabin in the middle of the tangerine field.
The people who were doing JukGwa start to migrate toward the cabin
and eat lunch that my mother prepared.

It's a red ripe watermelon and corn with densely embedded ears.
I've been following my grandmother around busily since this morning,
so it seems like the most delicious thing in the whole world.

"참 먹읍서!"
귤밭 가운데 오두막에서 엄마가 불러요.
적과를 하던 사람들이 오두막으로 모여
엄마가 준비한 **중석**을 먹지요.

빨갛게 익은 수박과 알이 촘촘히 박힌 옥수수예요.
아침부터 바쁘게 할머니를 따라다녔더니
세상에 이렇게 맛있는 건 또 없을 거예요.

We must hurry.
When the sun rises to the top of your head
as it becomes the afternoon,
the day gets so hot that we can't work.
Once again, people scatter out into the tangerine field.

서둘러야 해요.
오후가 되어 해가 머리 한가운데로 떠오르면
날이 더워져 일하기 힘들거든요.
사람들은 다시 귤밭으로 흩어져요.

I lie down in the cabin and look up at the sky.
It looks like if white oreums are gathered in the blue and deep sky.
Let's try jumping on top of that.
Mt.Halla over there and Seongsan Ilchulbong on this side!
Rise and fall! There's also a dragon's eye Oreum.
Leap! Run in stride.

나는 오두막에 누워 하늘을 보아요.
파랗고 깊은 하늘엔 흰 오름들이 모여 있는 것 같아요.
그 위를 뛰어올라 봐요.
저쪽에 한라산, 이쪽엔 성산 일출봉!
오르락내리락 용눈이오름도 있어요.
풀쩍! 한걸음에 뛰어올라 봐요.

"Hey, Haein!"
I open my eyes to someone's call.
I can barely see the shining sun behind
my uncle's back. Uncle Big Hands is here.

Because my uncle does stonewall work,
people call him Dolchengi(stone man).
He always handles a lot of rough stones,
so his hands are very coarse.
But I still like my uncle's big hands.
With my uncle's own hands,
a pretty stone wall is formed.

"얘, 해인아!"
누가 부르는 소리에 눈을 떠 보니
삼촌 등 뒤로 반짝이는 해가 보일락 말락.
왕손 삼촌이 왔어요.

돌담 쌓는 일을 하는 삼촌을 사람들은 **돌챙이**라고 불러요.
거친 돌을 많이 만져서 손이 우락부락하답니다.
그래도 나는 삼촌의 큰 손이 참 좋아요.
삼촌의 손길이 지나가면 예쁜 돌담이 생기거든요.

Small stones, big stones, ugly stones, round stones
It's amazing to see everything fitting into place.
There's nothing wasted.

My uncle is a stone wall artist.
Today, he fixed my grandmother's Chukkdam (stone wall).

The Chukkdam (stone wall) that surrounds the house,
goes well with the beautiful flowers my grandmother planted.
I really like my grandmother's yard
and this old house.

작은 돌, 큰 돌, 모난 돌, 둥근 돌
모두 자리를 찾아가는 것을 보면 **신기해요**.
버릴 것이 하나 없지요.

삼촌은 돌담 예술가예요.
오늘은 할머니 댁의 무너진 **축담**을 고쳤어요.

집을 둘러싼 축담은 할머니가 가꾼 예쁜 꽃나무들과
아주 잘 어울려요. 나는 할머니의 마당과
오래된 이 집이 참 좋아요.

My dad said that he is going to give me a special gift tonight.
I wonder what kind of present it will be?
I walked through the night forest while holding hands
with my mom and dad. "Shh! Now we have to be quiet.
You have to be very very careful when you get your gift from dad."
My dad says softly.

오늘 밤엔 아빠가 나에게 특별한 선물을 줄 거래요.
무슨 선물일까요? 엄마, 아빠와 손을 잡고 밤 숲을 걸어요.
"쉿! 지금부터 조용히 해야 해.
아빠가 줄 선물은 아주 조심조심 받아야 하거든."
아빠가 아주 작은 목소리로 말해요.

The beneath my feet crunch with a crisp sound.
The faint scent of honeysuckle wafs around my ankles.
I hear the buzz of small bugs flying around the grass.

At first, I don't see anything.
Slowly, I can make out the form of trees and I dimly see the roads too.
The crescent moon thinly smiles in a distance.

서걱서걱 발밑에서 부서지는 흙 알갱이
낮게 발목을 휘감는 인동꽃 향기
풀벌레들의 날개 비비는 소리

처음에는 아무것도 보이지 않더니
서서히 나무도 보이고 길도 어슴푸레 보이기 시작해요.
멀리 초승달이 가늘게 웃어요.

It was then.
One by one, small beams of light come from somewhere.

Sparkle
Sparkle
Sparkle

Small lights sparkle in front of my eyes.

그때였어요.
어디서 하나둘 작은 빛 알갱이가 다가와요.

반짝
반짝
반짝

눈앞이 조그만 빛들로 반짝여요.

Wow!
Before I can react, it flies out from the grass,
and the star embroidered black night dances in front of my eyes.
"It's called a Dochaebibul. You can only see it on a summer night."
I was shining together with the little beams of light
that shone brightly in the dark forest.

와하!
어느새 풀숲에서 가득 날아올라 검은 밤을 **펠롱** 수놓은
별빛들이 내 눈앞에서 춤을 춰요.
"**도채비불**이라는 거야. 여름밤에만 볼 수 있지."
나는 캄캄한 숲에서 환하게 피어오르는 그 작은 빛 알갱이와
함께 빛나고 있었어요.

"Dad, why are the Dochaebibul only in the deep woods?"

"I used to see them in front of my house when I was young.
But these days, there are many buildings.
and many of the forests are gone, so we can't see them that well.
Now you can only see the Dochabibul in a clear and unpolluted Gokgawal."

"아빠, 왜 도채비불은 깊은 숲속에만 있어요?"

"옛날에 아빠 어렸을 적에는 집 앞에서도 봤었단다.
그런데 요즘엔 건물이 많이 생기고,
숲도 많이 사라져서 잘 보이지 않아.
도채비불은 맑고 오염되지 않는 **곶자왈**에서만 볼 수 있게 되었지."

Lying down in bed, I close my eyes.
Thinking of the little densely sparkling stars that I saw in the woods.

The light of the dochaebi goes up into the dark night sky.
Then, it comes back down to my grandmother's tangerine field
and gets firmly stuck in the tangerine.

Ah~ Now I think I know.
Why my grandma's tangerines are so delicious!
I'm already looking forward to the sweet and sour winter!

잠자리에 누워 눈을 감아요.
숲에서 보았던, 촘촘히 빛나는 작은 별들을 생각해요.

도채비 불빛들이 밤하늘로 올라가 어두운 하늘을 가득 채워요.
그리고 다시 할머니 귤밭으로 내려와 귤 속에 콕콕 박혀요.

아~ 이제 알 것 같아요.
할머니 귤이 맛있는 이유를요!
벌써 새콤달콤 겨울이 기다려지는걸요!

Word Explanation

Gotjawal: Got means forest in Jeju, and Jawal means thorn bush. It's a primeval forest that is composed of a mixture of trees, vines, and plants where lava once flowed.

Nang: It's the Jeju Dialect for trees. For instance, "Nang swings are very fun" means that the "tree swings are very fun".

Dochaebibul: It's Jeju Dialect for fireflies. It is also called beullangi. In the old days, most of the fireflies that were seen on rice paddies and streams were called Ae Fireflies. They live in clean water, become adults by growing from eating marsh snails and snails, and flies for two weeks after reaching adulthood. But these days, as the environment becomes polluted, the Ae Fireflies are rapidly disappearing. You can only see it at Gotjawal on Jeju Island. The fireflies that live on Jeju are Unmunsan fireflies and Neuk fireflies, which can be seen in mid-June and mid-September. Jeju fireflies are said to show up around the early evening and light up the darkness.

Dolchengi: It's the Jeju dialect that means stone mason. A person who has a folk knowledge of stones is called a Dolchengi on Jeju Island. Dolchengis make all kinds of living tools out of stones, from stone walls to stone harubangs, milestone worked by horses and to pots used to carry water. Stones are the easiest things to see on Jeju Island, and have an inseparable relationship with the place. There are various types of stone walls, such as field walls that protect or separate fields, house walls and Oledams built to prevent strong winds from blowing into the house, and san walls, which are the fences of tombs.

Byuchida: it means lack of, be beyond one's capacity in Jeju Dialect. For instance, "my body was byucha so I can't do jump ropes" means that "my body is too tired, so I can't do jump rope."

Waarang Waarang: It refers to things that are hanging or gathered in abundance in Jeju Dialect.

JukGwa : It is the action of picking out fruits from trees that have too many fruits to protect the trees and get good fruits.

Jong-ae: It means knee in Jeju Dialect. For instance, "my Jong-ae hurts while I was climbing" means that "my knee hurts while I was climbing"

Jungseok: In Jeju, the meal that workers eat between breakfast and lunch is called Jungseok. It is assumed to be derived from the meaning of the Chinese words forbetween and meal. "Jetgulryum" is written to have the same meaning in the Jeju Big Dictionary.

Chukkdam : It's a stone wall that fences the house.

Pellong: It means "sparkle" in Jeju Dialect.

낱말 풀이

곶자왈: 곶은 제주어로 숲을 뜻하며, 자왈은 가시덤불을 의미해요. 용암이 분출되었던 곳에 나무, 덩굴식물 들이 뒤섞여 이루어진 원시림이지요.

낭: 나무의 제주어랍니다. 예를 들어 제주어로 "낭 그네 잘도 재미지다이"는 "나무 그네 되게 재미있다"라는 뜻이에요.

도채비불: 반딧불이의 제주어입니다. 불란지라고도 해요. 옛날에 주로 논이나 개울가에서 봤던 반딧불이는 대부분 '애반딧불이'였어요. 깨끗한 물에 살면서 다슬기나 달팽이 등을 먹고 자란 뒤 성충이 되어 2주간 날아다니지요. 그러나 요즘에는 환경이 오염되면서 애반딧불이가 많이 사라졌습니다. 제주도에서도 곶자왈에서만 만날 수 있어요. 제주에 서식하는 반딧불이는 운문산반딧불이와 늦반딧불이로, 6월 중순과 9월 중순에 볼 수 있습니다. 제주 반딧불이는 초저녁부터 모습을 드러내어 어둠을 밝힌다고 해요.

돌챙이: 석수의 제주도 방언입니다. 돌에 관한 민속 지식을 보유한 사람을 제주도에서는 돌챙이라고 불러요. 돌챙이는 돌담에서부터 돌하르방, 말방애, 물허벅에 이르기까지 돌로 온갖 생활 도구를 만들지요. 돌은 제주도에서 가장 쉽게 볼 수 있는 생활 재료이며, 그만큼 제주도와 떼려야 뗄 수 없는 관계입니다. 돌담의 종류가 다양한데, 밭을 보호하거나 구분 짓는 밭담, 집 안으로 몰아치는 강풍을 막기 위해 쌓은 집담과 올레담, 무덤의 울타리인 산담 등으로 구분하고 있어요.

버치다: 부치다, 버겁다는 뜻의 제주어예요. 예를 들어 "몸이 너미 버쳔 줄넘기 못허크라"는 "몸이 너무 힘들어 줄넘기 못하겠어"라는 뜻이지요.

와랑와랑: 사물이 풍성히 매달리거나 모여 있는 것을 말하는 제주어예요.

적과: 나무를 보호하고 좋은 과실을 얻기 위하여, 너무 많이 달린 과실을 솎아내는 일이에요.

종애: 무릎이라는 뜻의 제주어입니다. 예를 들어 "올라갈 때난 종애 아파수다"는 "올라갈 때 무릎이 아팠습니다"라는 의미예요.

중석: 일꾼들이 아침과 점심 사이에 먹는 밥을 제주에서는 중석이라고 해요. 끼니 사이(中)의 음식(中)을 뜻하는 한자어에서 변한 말로 짐작된답니다. 《제주어큰사전》에는 같은 뜻으로 '젯구름'이라 나와 있어요.

축담: 집을 둘러싼 돌담이에요.

펠롱: '반짝'을 뜻하는 제주어예요.

What kind of place is Jeju Island?

Jeju Island is the only volcanic island in Korea that is located in the range of 126° 08'~126° 58' E and 33° 06'~34° oo N'. The island's shape is an oval, and Mt. Halla is in the middle. It was designated as a World Natural Heritage in 2007, a World Cultural Heritage Site in 2009, and was certified as a World Geopark in 2010, making the entirety of Jeju Island one of the human cultural heritage keepers. At the top of Mt. Halla, the highest mountain in Korea, there is Baeknokdam which has a pool of water. There are also about 360 parasitic volcanoes called Oreum. Some of the representative Oreums are Seongsan Ilchulbong, Songaksan Mountain, Doosanbong Peak, Dangsan Peak, and Sanbangsan Mountain. There's also a lava cave. Caves such as the Manjang Cave, Gimnyeong Cave, Hyeopjaegul Cave, Ssangryong Cave, etc are examples of this kind of lava cave. The climate consists of a warm oceanic climate throughout the year and has very little fluctuation year-round.

There are many historically meaningful places on Jeju Island. The historic site of the Hangpaduri is famous for the Sambyolcho movement during the Goryeo Dynasty. It's also an island with a lot of painful history. It suffered a lot under the Japanese Empire in the Japanese Imperial era. As many as 3,500 fortified caves have been built all over Jeju to serve as military key points. The April 3 incident is also a great pain for Jeju. The April 3 incident is the incident where innocent people were killed in the process of the U.S. military government's suppression on the Namro Party of Jeju Island, who opposed the establishment of a single government in South Korea. There were reported to be up to 14,000 deaths at that time. So, if you travel Jeju Island, you can see the April 3 historic sites and memorial monuments for the victims strewn throughout. Jeju April 3 Peace Park was built to honor the victims on that day

What is representative of Jeju Island? The first are rocks. Jeju Island is an island made of rocks created by volcanic eruptions, so there are many rocks. If you go around Jeju Island, you'll commonly find stone houses, stone walls, stone warehouses, etc. And we can't forget about the volcanic rocks, the volcanic clay, the Jusangjeolli, that were formed as the volcano erupted. The second is the wind. As soon as you get off at the Jeju airport, you will first be greeted by the wind. It's very windy on Jeju Island. So even on very hot summer days, it feels cool in the shade, and in winter, even though the temperature isn't that low, it feels that way.

The third is the tangerines. In the winter of Jeju Island, tangerines are common. In any restaurant you go to, they serve tangerines for dessert. If you get to know your neighbor even a little on Jeju Island, you can get delicious tangerines throughout the winter. However, there are some difficulties in farming households in Jeju Island. Most of the tangerine farmers in Jeju Island are in their 60s or older. Most young people go to work in companies instead of trying to farm tangerines which are hard to do. That's why Jeju farming households lack a lot of working hands.

The fourth one is the forest. 61 percent of Jeju Island is composed of forests. So the air in Jeju is clear and the scenery is beautiful. Recently, too much reckless development has damaged Jeju Island and polluted the environment. It takes a lot of people's efforts to protect this beautiful natural heritage.

Haenyeo refers to a woman who goes into the ocean without any oxygen supply, and her job is to dig out the algae and shellfish. They are also called Jamnyeo are Jamsu. The culture of Jeju haenyeo was listed as a UNESCO intangible cultural heritage in 2016. The divers that harvest seafood throughout the world are mostly men. But in Jeju Island, strangely enough, the women do this job. Recently, the number of haenyeo in Jeju Island has decreased a lot. Those who are active still are mostly elderly grandma haenyeos.

We can't forget the food from Jeju Island, right? Jeju Island has many specialties such as Mom guk, meat noodles, Bingtteok and sea urchin seaweed soup. Mom Guk is a feast food where you fully boil pork and put seaweed fusiforme in the remaining water. Jeju Island residents have eaten pork since early times. That's why meat noodles that are made by putting chopped meat into a pork broth are famous. Bingtteok is a dish that rolls radish beef into a thin buckwheat pancake.

In addition, there is a shamanistic belief which is our native tradition on Jeju Island. Every spring, in February, we have Yeongdeungje, and around the onset of spring, we have Ipchungut in front of Gwandeokjeong, Gwana, Jeju-mok. Also, every year, villagers gather at the Songdang Main Hyangdang in a village called Songdang, to hold the Shingyaseje (January 14 on the lunar calendar), Yeongdeunggut (Feburay 14th), Maboolimje (July 14) and Simangokdaeje (October 14). Due to this, there are said to be 18,000 gods living on Jeju Island.

Currently, 670,000 people live on Jeju Island, and the population is increasing every year. Main Tourist attractions such as Mt Halla National Park, Seongsan Ilchulbong, Jeolmul Natural Recreation Forest, Jeju Olle Trail, Udo, Seopjikoji, Saryuni Forest Path, Hyeopjae Beach, Seogwipo Jungmun Tourist Park, Stone Culture Park, Sanbang Mountain, Songak Mountain, Saebyeol Oreum, Darangsh Oreum, etc. are crowded with tourists every day.

제주도는 어떤 곳?

제주도는 우리나라 유일의 화산섬이에요. 동경 126° 08´~126° 58´, 북위 33° 06´~34° 00´의 범위에 있는 우리나라에서 가장 큰 섬이에요. 섬의 모양은 타원형이고 가운데에는 한라산이 있지요. 2007년에 세계 자연유산, 2009년에 세계 문화유산으로 지정되었고, 2010년에는 세계 지질공원으로 인증을 받으면서 제주도 전체가 하나의 인류문화유산이 된 셈이에요. 남한에서 가장 높은 산인 한라산의 정상에는 백록담이 있으며 물이 고여 있습니다. 또 360여 개의 기생화산이 있는데 이를 오름이라고 합니다. 대표적인 오름으로는 성산 일출봉, 송악산, 두산봉, 당산봉, 산방산 등이 있습니다. 또 용암동굴도 있는데요, 만장굴, 김녕굴, 협재굴, 쌍룡굴 등이죠. 기후는 연중 온난하고 기온의 연교차가 적은 해양성 기후를 띠고 있지요.

제주도에는 역사적으로 의미 있는 곳이 많아요. 항파두리 유적지는 고려 때 삼별초 항쟁으로 유명한 곳입니다. 또 아픔을 간직한 섬이기도 해요. 일제 강점기에 일제로부터 많은 수난을 당했는데요, 군사적 요충지로 쓰기 위해 만든 진지동굴이 제주 전역에 3,500개나 된다고 합니다. 4·3 사건 또한 제주의 큰 아픔이에요. 4·3 사건은 미군정이 남한만의 단독정부 수립에 반대한 남로당 제주도당을 진압하는 과정에서 많은 무고한 주민이 희생된 사건입니다. 당시 사망자만 14,000여 명이었다고 해요. 그래서 제주를 여행하다 보면 곳곳에 4·3 유적지와 희생자 추모비를 만날 수 있습니다. 그 때의 희생자를 기리기 위하여 제주 4·3 평화공원이 만들어졌어요.

제주를 대표하는 것에는 무엇이 있을까요? 첫 번째는 돌이에요. 제주도는 화산 폭발로 인해 생겨난 돌로 만들어진 섬이라서 돌이 많아요. 제주를 다니다 보면 돌로 만든 집, 돌로 만든 담, 돌로 만든 창고 등을 흔히 볼 수 있답니다. 그리고 화산이 분출되면서 만들어진 화산암이나 화산송이, 주상절리도 빼놓을 수 없지요.

두 번째는 바람이에요. 제주 공항에 내리자마자 처음 만나는 것이 바람입니다. 제주도는 바람이 많이 불어요. 그래서 여름에는 몹시 더워도 그늘에만 들어가면 시원해요. 바람 때문에 겨울에는 기온이 그리 낮지 않아도 추위가 크게 느껴지지요.

세 번째로 귤이 있지요. 제주의 겨울에는 귤이 흔해요. 식당에 가면 어디서나 후식으로 귤을 제공해요. 제주에서 이웃과 조금만 친해지면 겨우내 맛있는 귤을 얻어먹을 수 있어요. 그런데 제주의 농가에도 힘든 점이 있답니다. 귤 농사를 지으시는 분 대부분은 60대 이상의 연로하신 분들이에요. 젊은 사람들은 힘든 귤 농사를 지으려고 하지 않고 회사에 다니는 경우가 많아요. 그래서 제주 농가에는 일손이 부족해요.

네 번째는 숲이에요. 제주 면적의 61%는 숲으로 이루어져 있어요. 그래서 제주도의 공기가 맑고 풍경도 아름다워요. 최근에 무리한 난개발로 풍광이 훼손되고 환경도 오염되고 있지요. 아름다운 자연 유산을 지키기 위해 많은 사람의 협조가 필요합니다.

다섯 번째는 해녀입니다. 해녀는 바닷속에 산소 공급 장치 없이 들어가 해조류와 패류를 캐는 일을 직업으로 삼는 여성을 말해요. 잠녀(潛女)·잠수(潛嫂)라고도 하지요. 제주 해녀 문화는 2016년 유네스코 인류무형문화유산으로 등재되었어요. 해산물을 수확하는 다른 나라의 다이버는 대부분 남성이에요. 그러나 제주에서는 특이하게도 여성이 그 일을 하지요. 최근 해녀가 많이 줄어들었어요. 그나마 활동하는 해녀 대부분은 연로한 할머니 해녀에요.

제주의 음식도 빼놓을 수 없겠지요. 제주도에는 몸국, 고기 국수, 빙떡, 성게 미역국 같은 별미가 많아요. 몸국은 돼지고기를 푹 고아 우린 물에 톳을 넣어 먹는 잔치 음식이에요. 제주도는 옛날부터 돼지고기를 먹었어요. 그래서 돼지고기 국물과 고기를 저며 얹은 고기 국수가 유명하답니다. 빙떡은 얇게 부친 메밀전병 안에 무로 만든 소를 넣어 돌돌 말은 음식이에요.

이 밖에도 제주도에는 우리나라의 전통인 무속신앙이 살아있어요. 해마다 봄이 되는 2월에는 영등제를 하고 입춘을 전후로 제주목 관아 관덕정 앞에서 입춘굿을 크게 해요. 또 송당 본향당에서는 매년 마을 사람들이 모여서 신과세제(음력 정월 14일)와 영등굿(2월 14일), 마불림제(7월 14일), 시만곡대제(10월 14일)를 올려요. 이를 빌어 제주에는 1만 8천 신이 산다고 합니다.

현재 제주도에는 67만 명이 거주하며 해마다 인구가 늘고 있어요. 한라산 국립공원, 성산 일출봉, 절물자연휴양림, 제주올레길, 우도, 섭지코지, 사려니숲길, 협재해수욕장, 서귀포 중문관광단지, 돌문화공원, 산방산, 송악산, 새별오름, 다랑쉬오름 등의 주요 명소마다 관광객으로 북적거려요.

제주도는 어디에?

- 제주도는 대한민국의 남서쪽에 있는 우리나라의 가장 큰 섬이에요!